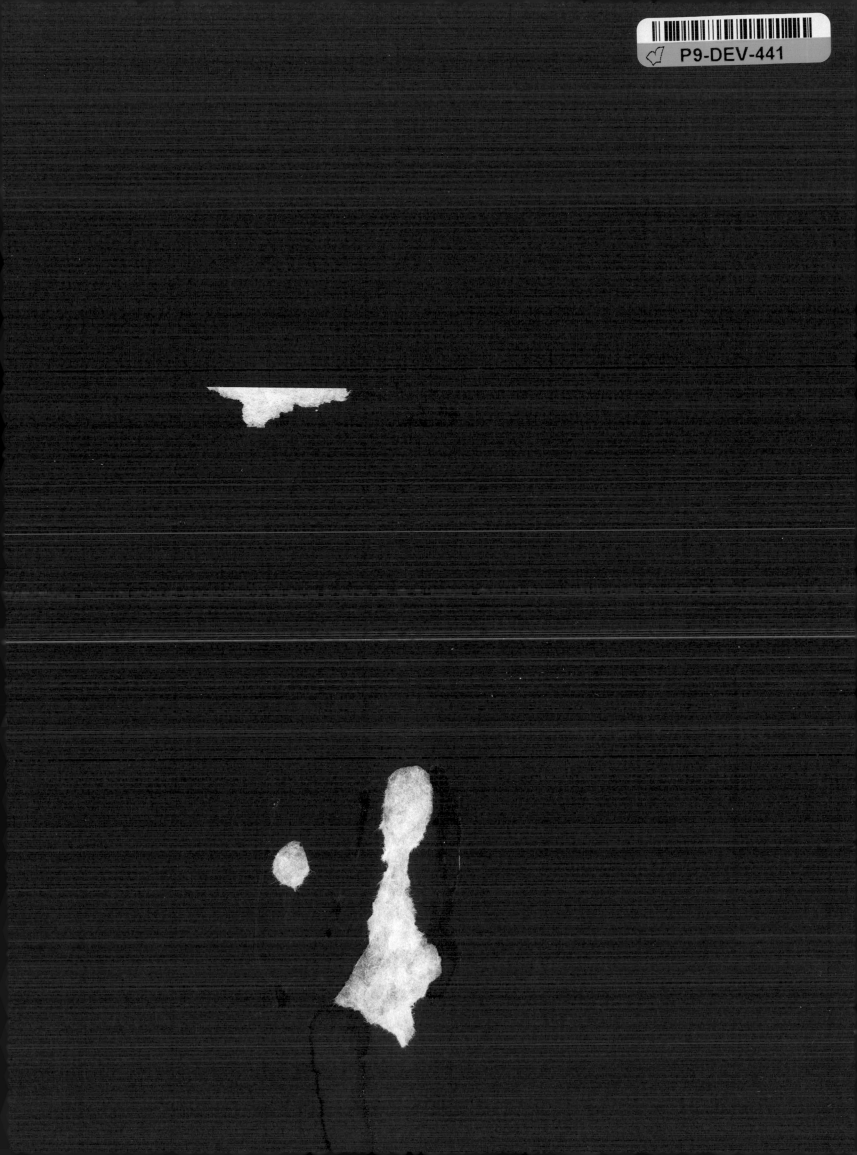

SUMMERTIME
Joe Baraban

'RENDEZVOUS HOUSTON,
A CITY IN CONCERT'

Ellis Vener

SAN JACINTO SUNSET
Joe Baraban

HOUSTON
A SELF-PORTRAIT

DESIGNED AND EDITED BY JERRY HERRING

TEXT BY DOUGLAS MILBURN

PHOTOGRAPHED BY
JOE AKER, JOE BARABAN, STEVE BRADY, JIM CALDWELL, FRED GEORGE,
DON GLENTZER, BOB GOMEL, MARK GREEN, JERRY HERRING, PAUL HESTER,
LEWIS HODNETT, JR., GEORGE O. JACKSON, JR., ROBB KENDRICK, ROCKY KNETEN,
KENT KNUDSON, CHRIS KUHLMAN, THAINE MANSKE, RALF MANSTEIN,
ARTHUR MEYERSON, JIM OLIVE, RICHARD PAYNE, J. LINDY POLLARD, JANICE RUBIN,
JACQUES DE SELLIERS, JIM SIMS, RON SCOTT, F. CARTER SMITH,
MARC ST. GIL AND ELLIS VENER

PRODUCED BY JERRY AND SANDY HERRING

PUBLISHED BY HERRING PRESS, HOUSTON

THE DOME

Arthur Meyerson

MEMORIAL PARK
Arthur Meyerson

SUNFISH ON CLEAR LAKE

Jim Sims

BLIMP BASE
Jim Sims

HOUSTON SHIP CHANNEL
Kent Knudson

RODEO TRAILRIDERS
Jim Olive

A self-portrait. The title occurred to me while editing the photographs that I had been collecting for months from Houston photographers. The body of work I was looking through had been shot on numerous locations around Houston for a variety of reasons, by a number of different photographers who had only one thing in common: they were photographing the city they live in. Their viewpoint is quite different from that of a visiting photographer. These are photos taken by people who sense the differences here. They understand the flow of the city. The light. The feel.

Ultimately, though, the view of the book becomes the editor's view, my view. What I brought to the project was a desire to show the Houston that I would share with a visitor. I am a proud owner of Houston. I like it here, and I like to show it off.

This is my point of view. It is a selective view, for sure. (And a view that ran out of pages, I might add.) Where are the slums, you ask. What about the freeways at rush-hour? Yes, these are part of the city, or any city for that matter. But that is not the point here. The point here is to celebrate what makes Houston different. What makes it a city that is as exciting to live in as it is to look at. What makes it a place that is loved.

–Jerry Herring

FOLK DANCERS
Janice Rubin

LOOKING WEST
FROM DOWNTOWN

Janice Rubin

UNDERSTANDING HOUSTON

THE GOLDEN AGE

Something happened to Houston on the way to the twenty-first century.

The first couple of decades I was in Houston, I pretty much ignored the city as city. It was a place to be, a town with little obvious sense of itself and no conscious vision of its place in history. A bayou town given to typical Texas boosterism, that now-vanished Houston was forever being one-upped by Dallas, which not only had more bank deposits but its own very successful opera company as well.

Now though, I find, the longer I am here, the harder it is to write about anything other than Houston. Every morning I get up and go out and the city takes me by the lapels and shakes me and says, look at this, and this, and this, isn't it extraordinary, have you ever seen anything like it? And I look and often I agree, it is extraordinary, and I've never seen anything quite like it.

Houston is not, to be sure, for everyone. The great cities never are. The message, fortunately, is now out, and pretty clear. You don't come here unless you are 1) bright, 2) creative, 3) a risk-taker, and 4) a workaholic. This city functions on a pure goal-standard. The catch is it's your goal, anything you choose. Set a modest goal and the chances are excellent you can attain it here. The ridiculous thing about Houston is that you can also set an outrageous goal, and the chances are excellent you can attain it here.

I laugh at Houston a lot. It is a city of constant surprises. Maybe that's the real secret of Houston – the people who stay are the ones who know how to laugh. I also, as you will see, take Houston very seriously. Like some huge American version of a complex Tibetan mandala, the city often functions as a centering device – a source of consolation and, possibly, a degree of enlightenment as well.

Sometimes I wonder if we don't all get together while we're asleep and have a big discussion about what kind of city we're going to "do" next. How else is one to explain the way Houston changes literally from day to day? The city as chameleon. It's not just the lack of zoning. It's as if the very air we breathe contains – in addition to the occasional pollutant – about 50 percent unpredictability.

Now here we are hurtling toward the Big Turning Point of the year 2000 and I don't know a city in the world as fecund, as mesmerizing, as nurturing, as exciting as Houston. The city of alchemy: a good-sized chunk of the world's wealth pours in here and we, somehow, transform that wealth into a late twentieth century version of Shangri-La. Energy city? Sure, and it's not just the oil. The energy is almost tangible; you sense it when you step off a plane.

The world does this occasionally – creates a place where we can do new things, and it's always up to the bright, creative risk-takers to make it happen. Others need not apply.

Kuala Lampur. Kyoto. Persepolis. Kashmir. Borobudur. Cairo. Venice.

Florence. Places that, because of what was done there, now belong to the world. They all share certain qualities: beauty, coherence, a feeling of profound tolerance, an almost arrogant sense of self-confidence. Like these places, Houston is a massive and daring act of imagination. This is no city for weak hearts and timid spirits.

It's happened twice in a big, consistent way before in this country, first in New York near the end of the last century, and then in Los Angeles in the early part of this century.

If you want to understand Houston, you've got to understand that we are here, next in line. The Greeks, with irony, called it hubris, pride, this drive to storm the gates of heaven. They knew it was dangerous. They also knew that when it starts happening, there is no stopping it, until the gods so will.

Of course some afternoons around 5:30 on the freeways it seems the gods have so willed. And no doubt there are more than a few ulcers riding around in limos as a result of whatever economic difficulties, whether it's falling oil prices, or unfilled office space, that the city happens to be passing through at the moment. Add to those recurring headaches the larger, more troublesome difficulties endemic to American capitalism (10 percent of the people living at the poverty level) and you have enough material to keep a platoon of economic and urban analysts employed for the foreseeable future. Houston's problems, which it to some degree shares with the country and the world, are not the point here. The point is that the city has developed a momentum which is carrying it – problems and all – toward a creative highground that few cities have occupied.

Look at the downtown skyline of an afternoon against a Gulf blue sky filled with a thousand impossibly friendly and fluffy white ships scudding past the last word from the 20th century on highrise beauty. Sharing that view with me, you'd have a hard time convincing me that the Golden Age of Houston has not begun. I know, I know. Such a thing here on the coastal plain of Texas? It's contrary to all reason and expectation. The city as we have it certainly doesn't fit the Texas, nor for that matter many of the American, stereotypes. What need have cowboys of an ocean anyhow, much less the largest international port in North America? But the paradox of Houston is in the best tradition of historical surprises. In a world still cowering before the antique fears of Chaos and Old Night, Houston has embarked on a bold adventure which puts it in a very select group of cities, and eras.

Upstart? Superficial? Chaotic? Provincial? Immature? Nonsense. I've lost patience with those people who come here and go away yelping about how we're not another New York or London or Paris. Of course we're not. The world loves to repeat itself, but never in such a literal manner.

Houston is what it will be. And it is not some urbanologist-architect-critic's private little vision of the Ideal City.

People get the kind of city they want, and deserve. You wind up living in a given city because you are drawn by the personality of that city. A certain group of Americans was strongly attracted to Paris in the 1920s, because of what Paris was. A different group of Americans at the same time was attracted to Berlin, because Berlin was something else. Those are the spectacular examples. A similar, lower-key attraction applies to smaller, more modest cities and their smaller populations. You don't, for example, move to Portland if you want to be surrounded by artistic, scientific, or commercial genius. You move to Portland, well, for whatever reason it is that people move to Portland.

We, here, are in the process of making the kind of city we deserve, and want. And it's a knock-out. If you begin studying cities of the past, looking for parallels, there's one that jumps out at you. Houston is what you get if you do Florence 500 years later. Same energy. Same "chaos." Same creativity.

Of course it doesn't look like Florence. If you're in need of exact duplications of what has come before, visit Williamsburg. Or Disney World. The antiseptic past that so many people revere has powerful charms. What is forgotten is that what you see in Florence today is creativity *preserved*. What you see in Houston is creativity *in process*. Houston is the real thing. It is not neat, it is not tidy. It is the miracle of the lotus: from the mud through murky water a stalk rises which, upon reaching air, gives the world a flower without equal.

Birth is messy. And painful. No one seems to know quite why, but it is. Of course, the mere existence of a painful mess does not necessarily imply birth. It may imply only the existence of a painful mess. I look at Houston and I see a painful mess, but I also see the miracle of birth: a young, outrageously luxurient tropical tree bearing extraordinary fruit on the third coast of America.

Beware the sterile mind that fears the creative process. It's always the same and, to the unperceptive outsider, it always looks chaotic. Henry Ford's first workshop. Rembrandt's studio. Eisenstein's movie sets. What kind of a housekeeper do you think Beethoven was? You only get the Florence we think of as "Florence" or the Venice we think of as "Venice" when you've had several centuries to clean up after the big creative explosion.

At the height of its Renaissance glory, Florence stank, and it was always flooding. Moreover, Florence was a "one-industry" town. The industry? Wool. Those crazy people in Central Italy didn't know that it was absurd to try to turn a little Italian river town that was constantly being flooded into one of the world's great cities by importing, processing, and selling one product. Since they were unaware that this was impossible, they did it. So uppity did this little town become that they even founded their own republic.

The Florentines were furthermore alchemists. They turned vision into work, work into wealth, and – the hardest of all – wealth into beauty. The Strozzi family, for example, spent twenty years acquiring parcels of land before beginning construction of one of the marvels of Florentine architecture, the Strozzi Palace. If that sounds familiar it's because the Menil family is doing precisely the same thing right now in the Montrose. Having assembled the land, the Menil Foundation has now constructed a museum to house the Menil Collection. The unique circumstances and means and people necessary for such private visions made real do not come together very often.

Not only did Florence smell bad, it was at that time a half-built, unfinished mess. The great cathedral, the Duomo, had been started in 1296. The design included a dome of such a great span (149 feet) that no one had been able to figure out how to build it. After 130 years, the structure was finished, except for the gaping hole where the dome was to be. In the 1420's the city held a competition to find a solution. A young architect by the name of Filippo Brunelleschi, breathing the brute optimism that must have permeated that unpleasant Florentine air, tackled the problem, and won the contest. In 1436 Florence celebrated the completion of its domed cathedral.

It's hard to say who scoffed more, the bankers or the structural engineers, in the 1950's when Roy Hofheinz went public with his dream of a domed stadium. Yet there the Astrodome stands today, a translucent jewel which none of the countless subsequent imitations has quite matched.

Why Houston? Why, for that matter, Florence? There in the Piazza stands Michelangelo's *David*. Why there? I don't know, but it probably is the same reason why the city produced a Brunelleschi who could figure out how to build a dome there such as the world had never seen.

The collection of monumental architecture that Houston has put up in the last 20 years doesn't just happen. Not on such a scale of exquisitely reasoned quality. It takes a special time, a special place, and unusual people. What Houston is doing costs a great deal of money and the burden of proof is on the naysayer to convince me that the business people who are building these Houston monuments are not in the grip of the same creative forces that earlier, and on a much smaller scale, gave us Florence.

And maybe we're through. Maybe the architecture is all. Maybe Galveston, whose lovely collection of 19th century architecture was frozen in time following the 1900 storm, is an omen. Perhaps Houston is to be a huge frozen-in-time museum of late 20th century architecture.

Maybe, but I don't think so. To understand why not, we have next to explode the biggest Houston myth, the one our critics, both foreign and home-grown, are fondest of, namely, the myth that this is a city without a past.

The truth is, again, simple. There will, I believe, be more than architecture here, because this city, whether we are conscious of it or not, is in the grip of and controlled by a past that is richer, more powerful, and more intensely accessible than that of most any city in the world. The past always shapes us, and incredible Houston is a direct product of an incredible history.

THE CITY IN HISTORY

Something keeps drawing me back to the San Jacinto Battleground, always in the afternoon. Is it perhaps because the solution to the mystery of Houston is here?

What an unlikely spot for one of the world's decisive battles. Tending toward marsh, the country here is laced with inlets and bayous and streams too small for naming. The vegetation is coastal scrub dotted with stands of live oak. You can tell which of the trees are old, native growth and which have been planted. The old trees are stunted and lean tiredly away from the prevailing Gulf winds.

Here Sam Houston camped, knowing that Santa Anna was just a few miles away toward Galveston. The Mexican general was trying to catch the rebel Texas government–he had almost got them at Harrisburg, and just missed them at Morgan's Point on the bay. After capturing the elected officials, Santa Anna planned to mop up the troublesome little Texas army.

For two weeks, Houston had been leading the Republic's troop of some 700 tired and poorly equipped men across 200 miles of southeast Texas. These were not ordinary people, and at least some of them must have known they were doing something quite extraordinary. One of Houston's officers, Capt. John M. Allen, was a soldier of fortune and man of learning; he had been at Byron's side when the poet died in Greece in 1823. Houston himself had two books with him during the campaign. *Gulliver's Travels,* and Caesar's *Gallic Wars.* In his head, he had Homer. When, as a boy, Sam went to live with the Cherokees, he took – and memorized large sections of – Pope's translation of *The Iliad.*

The weather that spring of 1836 was awful. Incessant rains had turned the few primitive roads into quagmires, and it had been an unusually cold April. With a strong norther blowing, the temperature on the morning of the 21st was in the low forties.

Sam Houston, general of the army of the Republic of Texas, slept late and – Robert Penn Warren says – when he woke up the first thing he saw was an eagle circling overhead. There had been two other eagle-omens in his life, the first when, leaving Tennessee with a broken heart following his failed marriage, he crossed the Cumberland, and then again when he had crossed the Red River to enter Texas.

The Texans had wanted to fight many times, but Houston kept his own counsel. Was it his Indian smarts? He lived with the Cherokees twice, as a boy in Eastern Tennessee for two years and then he spent three years with them in Oklahoma after the failure of his marriage. What did he learn from them? Patience, surely. How amazing that he could wait so long to engage his enemy. Cunning? Perhaps. On April 20 the Texans camped due west of the Mexicans. When Houston finally gave the order to attack late on the afternoon of the 21st, the Mexicans had the sun directly in their eyes.

The Texas army, for all its makeshift quality, had a band. As they attacked, a fife and drum played an English lovesong, "Will You Come to the Bower?"

You dream. You plan and prepare. You wait, looking for the right time and place. And then you risk everything. When you win, you get all the marbles. The specific nature of what you win depends on what you have put at risk, and what your dream was. Sam won a large piece of North America, plus a new nation, and – though he didn't know it at the time – a startling new city that lately has finally been showing some signs of at last being worthy to bear his name.

There is a grove of trees where the Mexican camp was, with stone markers showing the location of Santa Anna's tent, the Mexican breastworks, the Mexican cannon. In the field toward the monument is another marker: "Houston wounded and horse killed under him in battle."

This is where the battle happened, not in the more easily accessible Texan camp, which is on the bank of Buffalo Bayou. Where the Texans waited it's hard to imagine the scene – the bayou is now a ship channel, the land has been graded, a levee has been built. But at the site of the Mexican camp, along toward the middle of the afternoon when the cicadas start to sing and the wind picks up a bit through the old oak trees, it's easy to imagine that army of impatient Texans bursting out of the low scrub and surprising their enemy. The Mexicans got off only three shots from their cannon. Santa Anna himself was apparently dallying with his mistress. Within minutes, the battle turned into a rout that lasted until evening as the Texans pursued and slaughtered the defeated Mexican army.

Revenge – for the Alamo, and Goliad? No doubt that was in the Texans' minds. And the Mexicans paid a dear price – more than 600 dead and 700 taken prisoner while only eight Texans were killed. But Houston again confounded his compatriots: he refused to execute Santa Anna. So, to dreaming, planning, and patience must be added mercy. Though, in this case, Houston's mercy was no doubt strongly affected by political considerations. Santa Anna was a valuable hostage for the new and highly vulnerable infant nation to hold.

The inscription on the base of the monument that was erected a hundred years later reads: "Measured by its results, the Battle of San Jacinto was one of the decisive battles of the world. The freedom of Texas from Mexico won here led to annexation and to the Mexican War, resulting in the acquisition by the United States of the states of Texas, New Mexico, Arizona, Nevada, California, Utah, and parts of Colorado, Wyoming, Kansas, and Oklahoma. Almost one-third of the present area of the American nation, nearly a million square miles, changed sovereignty."

If you want to understand the city, Houston, you have to understand the man, Houston. In an age when this country produced more than its share of larger-than-life figures, Sam was a giant. His presence still surrounds – and, I have come to believe, defines the city: San Jacinto; the Sam Houston Museum in Huntsville and his nearby grave; Cedar Point, south of Baytown where he had a house on Galveston Bay; the Sam Houston Library in Liberty. Then there is the little museum on Interstate 10 in Wallisville – they have a letter from Houston on display. Go there sometime and look at his signature. You can't miss it. It's large and florid. Look again, and you see that the way he signed his first name is ambiguous. You can read it either as "Sam Houston," or as "I am Houston."

In this age of media mediocrity, where leaders often have no more substance than the glowing electrons on a hundred million television screens, America lives on a mediocre level, and we forget that greatness is possible, and when it comes, is transcendent. With Sam Houston, we are in the presence of greatness.

Having as a young man already been a congressman and governor of Tennessee, he came here and created a country, with a million square miles – almost half a continent really. And then he worked to merge that country with the United States. After serving as president of the Republic of Texas, he was then elected U.S. senator for the new state. In the 1850's there was talk of his running for president, but his staunchly anti-slavery stance deprived him of a southern base of support. Coming home in 1860, he was elected governor. When intolerance reigned and Texas seceded, he resigned the governorship in disgust rather than rule with and over small-minded men.

A city without a past? What nonsense. The key to Houston, its very soul, is its history. Houston is a city overwhelmed by its past. Few cities have had such a powerful imprint placed on them from the beginning. Think about it: Rome didn't. The Romans had to invent myths (Romulus and Remus) about their beginnings. As did the Athenians.

But not us. We know how this place started. We know when and where it started, and we know who started it. Officially Houston was founded on August 30, 1836, by the Allen brothers where Buffalo and White Oak Bayous join, but Houston's real birth date is April 21, 1836, and the place of birth is San Jacinto. Go to the top of Transco Tower and look east. You will see another tower on the horizon, a slim 570-foot shaft of Texas limestone, reminding you where this town came from. Sure, we can pretend it's not there, that battlefield and that monument, and we can even forget what memories and whose spirit we invoke every time we write or say the name of the city. Our forgetfulness doesn't change the fact that Houston, like all cities, is a prisoner of its past. This unlikely place, this flat near-swamp by the tropical sea, is not its own master. The ghosts of heroes walk this city, and for their sake, I am impatient with those whose myopic vision tries to deny the once and future glory of Houston.

We've got his city, if not finished, at least pretty well underway. The only question remaining now is: what do we do with it?

CITY OF DREAMS

I live in the inner city in Houston, and I live in a forest. The trees are green year-round. It is not a perfect forest. There are, as in any forest, sinkholes here and there, places where things decay, where life, trying to renew itself, has to go through the ugly, painful processes of death and regeneration. But mostly it is a good forest. It is laced with curving, soaring strips of concrete. Some call the freeways scars. I don't. This forest is very forgiving, and very patient, very nurturing.

I simultaneously live in another forest. This one is new, and still being formed, still incomplete. It is a forest of visionary buildings. When I want to go somewhere, I get in a car, and the car takes me up and out of the green forest onto rising and falling views of human-made beauty – graceful, elegant, gleaming, curving, faceted visions of affirmation and hope. One of the truths of Houston is the profoundly supportive and encouraging daily visual effect of those towers rising out of the green forest.

For a long time Americans could dream anywhere. But, after an assassination in Dallas, a disastrous and tragic war in Vietnam, and a disgraced president, we seem to have forgotten or lost our ability to dream. Houston has not forgotten: the city of hope confounding the cynic, the city of affirmation confounding the pessimist, the city of dreams.

You want the moon? We gave you the moon. You want Mars? Coming up. And: Is it an accident that the first national women's meeting since Seneca Falls in 1848 was held in Houston? A day came in 1972 when the great-niece of Susan B. Anthony stood on the steps of the Convention Center and reminded us of her ancestor's most visionary and courageous words: "Failure is impossible."

You want more? Where, you say, is the Houston Dante, where the Houston Michelangelo? And I say, where indeed? Outlanders would do well to recall our Indian patience and our Indian cunning. A process was started here on April 21, 1836, and we're not quite done with it yet.

I think about the children of Houston, and I wonder what it must be like to grow up amidst such a visionary spectacle. There are already signs that the golden age will extend to the other arts – in painting, the Houston School is now part of the national art consciousness; and the number of Houston writers with a national audience continues to increase.

Houston has no proper reason to be here or to be what it is – other than 150 years of people dreaming ridiculous, outrageous, chaotic dreams, and then overcoming the obstacles and making those dreams real. Old Sam is one powerful role-model, let me tell you. John F. Kennedy knew as much, and his description of Sam's life in *Profiles in Courage* serves as the final summary of Sam's city: Houston the city, like Houston the man, is a baffling, fertile concoction of "indomitable individualism, sometimes spectacular, sometimes crude, sometimes mysterious, but always courageous."

– Douglas Milburn

Houston, though it retains a strongly focused downtown, has created a number of other centers, some quite
massive. It is not uncommon for visitors to arrive at one
of these centers on the edge of the city and stop, thinking
 they have reached Houston when in fact they still have
some miles to go. Urbanologists have a word for such a
city: polynucleated. But no matter how many secondary
centers it has developed – City Post Oak, Sharpstown,
the Energy Corridor, Highway 6, First Colony,
Greenspoint, The Woodlands, Clear Lake – Houston
has retained a strongly focused city center, which has
become even more dominant in the last 25 years. As a
place where many of the world's leading architects have
put up highrises, downtown Houston now represents
the purest, most cohesive collection of late twentieth
century skyscrapers in the world. Because of the scale of
the downtown street-grid – the blocks are 250′ by 250′,
each of the buildings occupies its own space, set slightly
apart from the others. The effect is that of a large number
of distinctive structures unified by proximity and a
shared quality of outstanding design.

SKYLINE FROM I-45
Steve Brady

NIGHT SKYLINE
Rocky Kneten

DOWNTOWN PANORAMA

The major buildings surrounding Sam Houston Park: RepublicBank Center, Texas Commerce Tower, Pennzoil Place, One Shell Plaza, Allied Bank Plaza, InterFirst Plaza, Allen Center One, Allen Center Two, MCorp Plaza, Four Allen Center and 1600 Smith in Cullen Center.

Lewis Hodnett, Jr.

SUNSET SKYLINE

George O. Jackson, Jr.

WEST HOUSTON SKYLINE

Looking west from near Hermann Park. The skylines of Greenway Plaza and City Post Oak appear to be one, although they are separated by nearly 4 miles.

George O. Jackson, Jr.

SAN JACINTO MONUMENT

Arthur Meyerson

Houston, to the world, is a mélange of oil, wealth, architecture, cowboys, space, and medicine. The symbols – the buildings, the people, the organizations, the activities – behind that image are neatly woven into the larger texture of the city. They define the city at the same time that they are defined by the city. Astronauts at Gilley's, art and cattle at the same auction, soaring monuments amidst the refineries – the symbols collide, combine, re-combine. The more the city of surprises changes the more it stays the same. It is these symbols which visitors expect to see – the Astrodome, NASA, the San Jacinto Monument, the skyscrapers, the man-made Ship Channel, the Texas Medical Center, River Oaks, the Rothko Chapel, and so on.

NASA TOURISTS

Jim Caldwell

ASTRODOME AT HALFTIME
Bob Gomel

TRANSCO FOUNTAIN

With this monument of aqueous filigree, architects Philip Johnson and John Burgee gave the city its own Niagara.

Steve Brady

**TRANSCO FOUNTAIN
WATER WALL**

Steve Brady

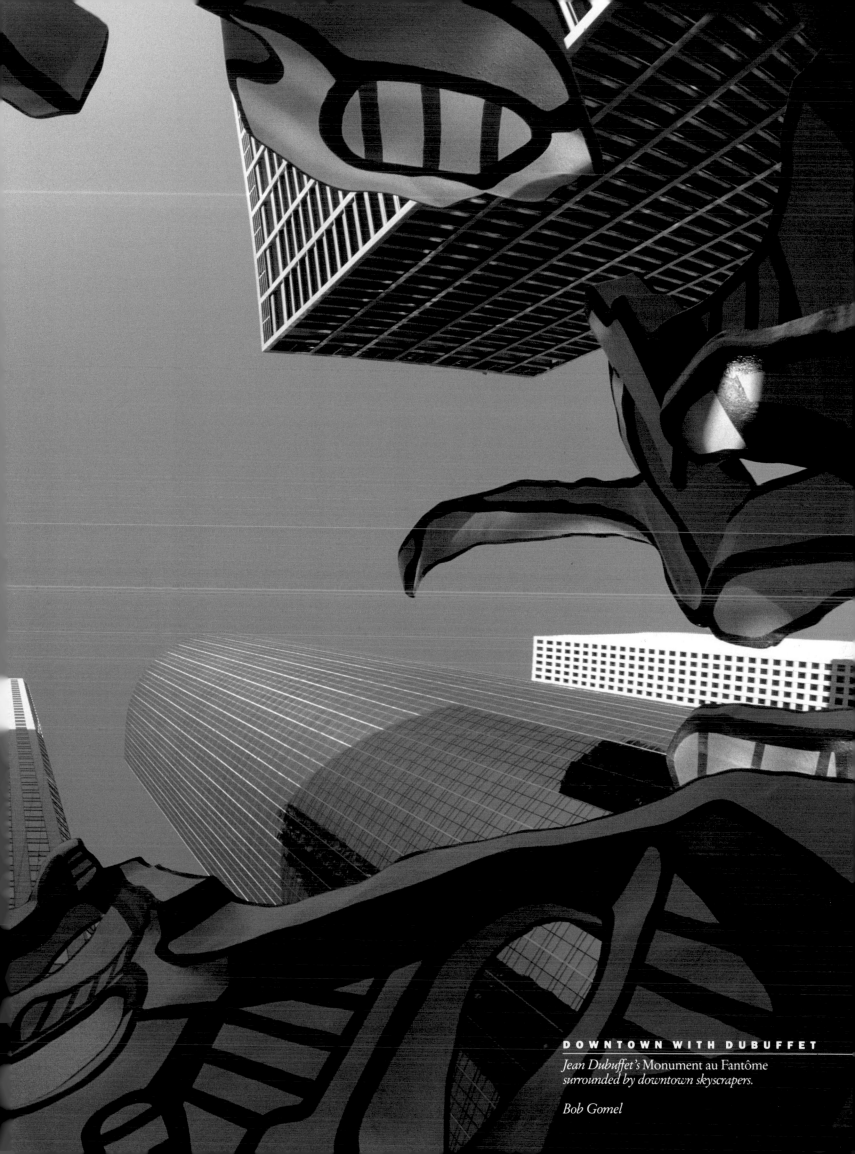

DOWNTOWN WITH DUBUFFET

Jean Dubuffet's Monument au Fantôme
surrounded by downtown skyscrapers.

Bob Gomel

RICE UNIVERSITY

Lovett Hall (1912) was the first building on the campus which now comprises 300 acres of heavily wooded inner city land.

Ron Scott

HERMANN HOSPITAL

Hermann Hospital opened its doors in 1924, the first building of what was to become the Houston Medical Center.

Steve Brady

BAYOU BEND

*The home of arts patron Miss Ima Hogg is now
The Bayou Bend Collection of American
Decorative Arts, a branch of The Museum of
Fine Arts.*

Jim Olive

GALLERIA

*The world famous shopping mall hurls
the gauntlet of a sky-lighted ice rink at the
Houston climate.*

Jim Sims

REFINERY

Ron Scott

PAGODA IN HERMANN PARK

The Houston forest, which conceals many wonders such as this Hermann Park pagoda – a gift from Taipei, elsewhere yields to a different forest of silver towers that make up the world's largest petrochemical complex.

Jim Sims

S U N S E T

George O. Jackson, Jr.

On the same latitude as Cairo and New Delhi, Houston has a quality of light, a white intensity which iridesces off the nearby sea and paints the vast Texas sky with colors that more somber climates can only dream about. Add sea fogs and sea storms from the warm Gulf waters and you get a city embraced by endlessly fickle and flattering skies – skies which, one must add, often seem impossibly vast. Houston sits on a very gently rolling coastal plain, which gives the city a distant, straight horizon-line that paradoxically confines and releases it at the same time. Because of NASA, Houston became known as Space City. But the visitor, roaming about in Houston's 600 square miles, usually develops another, more literal sense of space. The limitless Texas prairie combines with the huge bowl of sky to give the feeling that there is room enough – and, perhaps, time enough – here to accomplish just about anything you might desire.

SKYLINE AT SUNSET
Jim Olive

DOWNTOWN IN EARLY MORNING FOG

Jim Sims

SKYLINE IN THE FOG

George O. Jackson, Jr.

CITY IN THE RAIN

George O. Jackson, Jr.

CITY WITH A RAINBOW

George O. Jackson, Jr.

MORNING SKY

George O. Jackson, Jr.

EARLY MORNING OILFIELD IN SOUTH HOUSTON

Jim Sims

LONGHORN IN WEST HOUSTON SUNSET

Working ranches still exist on the edge of the city.

Jim Olive

GALLERIA COWBOY

Kent Knudson

Houstonians have built the most air-conditioned city in
the world. Like the British faced with the noonday Indian
sun, we flee the heat and humidity. It's no accident that the
first domed stadium was built here. Or that most downtown buildings are connected by a four-mile labyrinth
of pedestrian tunnels and underground malls. But the yin
of a steamy August is balanced by the yang of a balmy
winter. Which means that after the heat of mid-summer
is past, the city springs another of its surprises as its
air-conditioned populace moves outdoors – into the forest
of pines and live oaks that covers most neighborhoods,
to the beaches, the bays, and the ocean itself.

ROCKETS

Joe Baraban

PARTY

Bob Gomel

KINGWOOD NEIGHBORHOOD
Steve Brady

BEFORE THE GAME
Ralf Manstein

WATERSKIING AT
THE SHAMROCK

Bob Gomel

ON MONTROSE BOULEVARD

Jim Olive

ICE HOUSE

The ice house – an open-air neighborhood bar – is a southern tradition which led to convenience stores. Though the spin-offs are air-conditioned, the original ice houses remain stubbornly open to the elements.

Robb Kendrick

ON CLEAR LAKE

Jim Sims

**WEST HOUSTON
BALLOONISTS**

Thaine Manske

MIDNIGHT MADNESS
BIKE RACE

Once a year, in the wee hours of an October Sunday morning, thousands of Houston cyclists take over the streets for a grand tour of the city.

Robb Kendrick

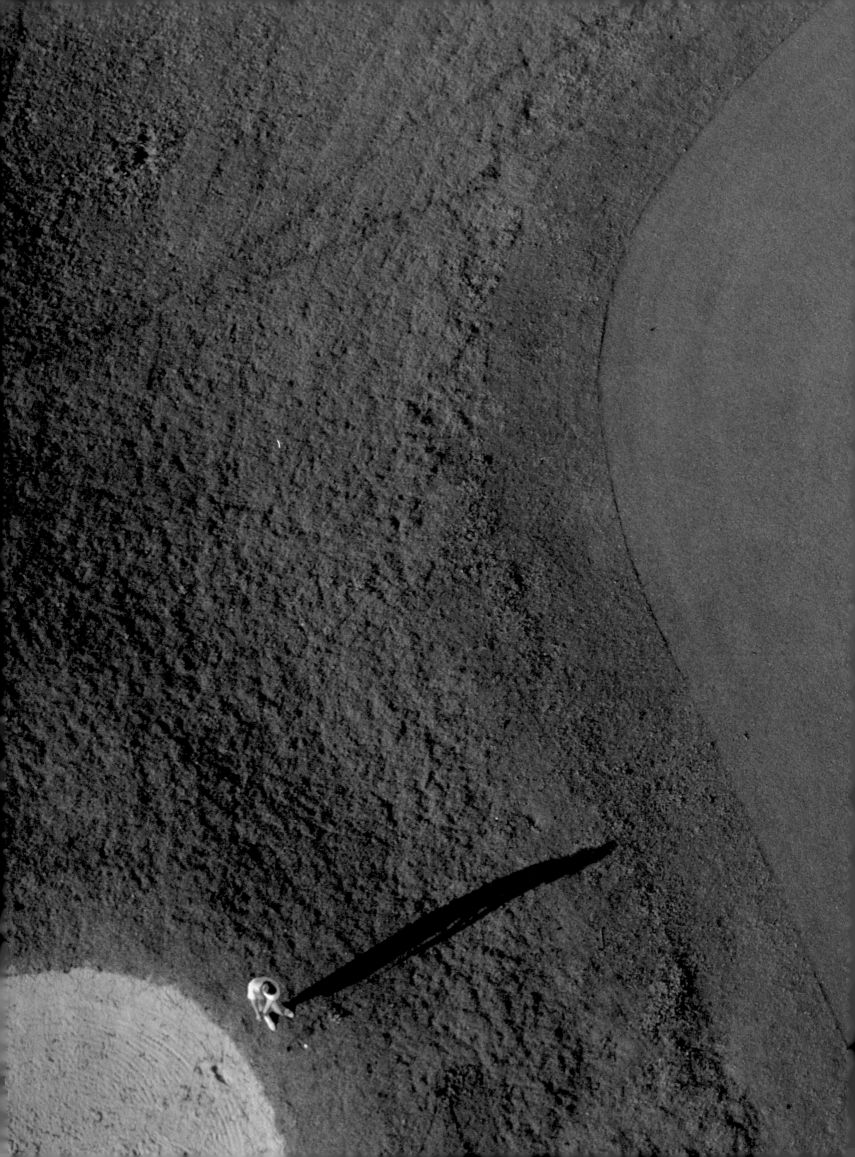

SOFTBALL PLAYERS
AT RICE

Jerry Herring

WALKING IN THE TREES

Jim Sims

GOODE COMPANY
BARBECUE
Janice Rubin

While there is some overlap between Texas stereotypes and Houston stereotypes, the city is better understood on its own, separate terms. As the largest international seaport in North America, Houston has attracted a population whose diversity is matched only by that of Los Angeles and New York City. Mix such a citizenry with the mild climate and you get a public scene that is informal, colorful, and often unpredictable – whether at the Houston Festival in the spring, the semi-annual Westheimer Arts Festival, the Clear Lake Regatta, Galveston Mardi Gras, the Houston-Tenneco Marathon, the Foley's Thanksgiving Parade, the Lunar New Year in Chinatown, the Rodeo Parade, Fiestas Patrias, or the Juneteenth Blues Festival in Hermann Park.

RICE BEER BIKE RACE

Jerry Herring

HOUSTON FESTIVAL

A two-week outdoor celebration of the arts.

Janice Rubin

GREAT WESTERN AUCTION

An annual sale of the best in cattle – and western art.

Bob Gomel

TRADE SHOW AT THE DOME

Bob Gomel

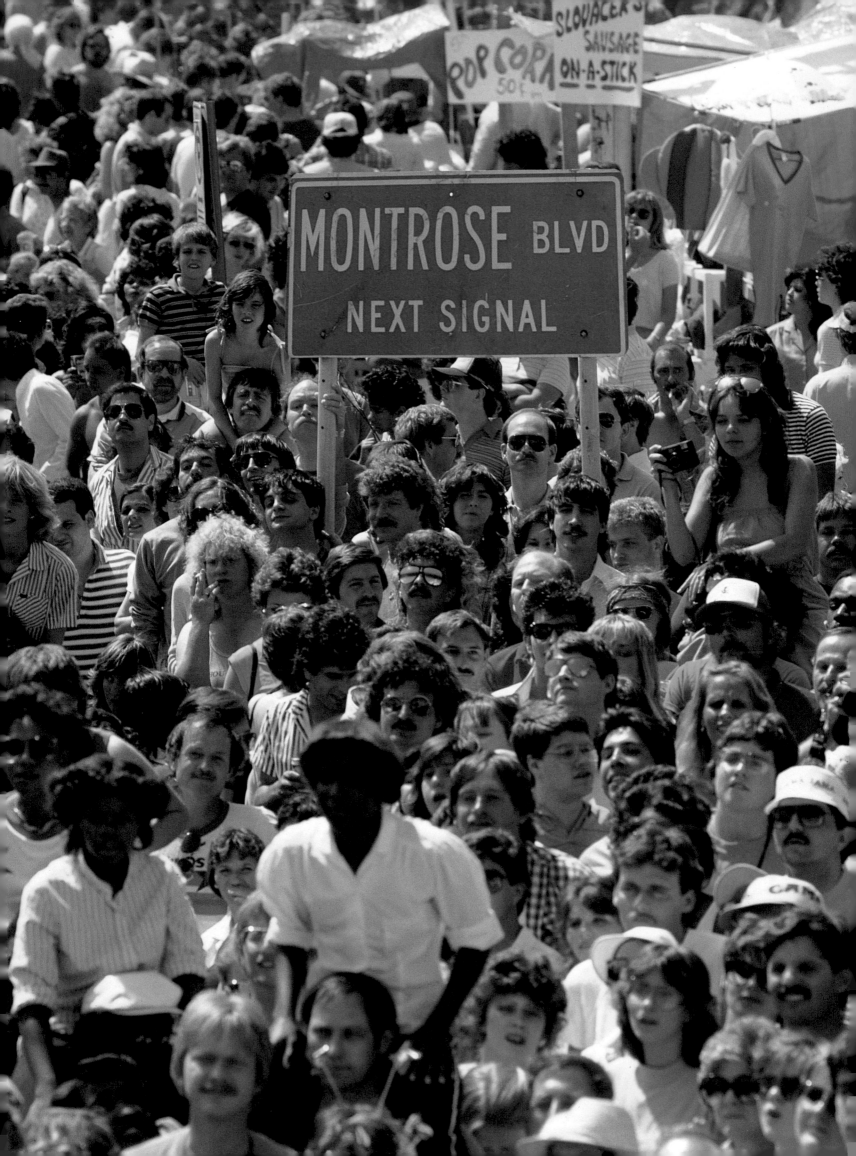

WESTHEIMER COLONY
ART FESTIVAL

*Each fall and spring, for one weekend, the heart
of the Montrose area becomes the place to see and
be seen.*

Mark Green

MARATHON ON
MEMORIAL DRIVE

The annual Houston–Tenneco Marathon.

Thaine Manske

MARATHON WINDING
THROUGH TOWN

Jim Olive

HOUSTON-TENNECO TENNECO
MARATHON

2:11:30
PLACE 1

MARATHON FINISH
Jim Olive

MILLER OUTDOOR THEATER

This hillside theater in Hermann Park is one of the city's true community centers, hosting an annual opera festival, summer symphony concerts, ballet performances, Juneteenth and Fiestas Patrias celebrations, and more – all free.

F. Carter Smith

CONCERT

Joe "King" Carrasco at Fitzgerald's.

F. Carter Smith

**LITTLE LEAGUE
PICTURE DAY**

*The annual springtime ritual, here at
the West University Little League field.*

Jerry Herring

The new city awaits its Margaret Mead who will help us understand what it's like to be a child in this urban environment like no other. Since no one has yet written a *Growing Up in Houston,* we can look for clues in these images of Houston children. Many of the children are here because their parents have discovered that Houston is an eminently livable city. Starting with the climate, which allows children to be outdoors as much and as often as they want to be, you proceed to the widespread child-amenities: a range of schooling from the most traditional to the most progressive, a first-rate zoo, a half-dozen beaches in easy driving distance, a transit system that has now developed into a model for the country, major cultural organizations with active outreach programs. One curious anthropological note: so thoroughly is Houston already encapsulated from its Texas outback that the children of the Bayou City grow up speaking a standard English untouched by the nearby regional accents of East and West Texas.

BACKYARD BARBECUE

Joe Baraban

BACKYARD
HOUSE PAINTERS

Jerry Herring

SWIM CLASS

Jim Sims

CHILDREN'S MUSEUM

Janice Rubin

**GIRL SCOUTS AT
GREENWAY PLAZA**

Joe Baraban

CLASSROOM

Janice Rubin

YOUNG VIOLINIST

Janice Rubin

FAMILY AT THE GALLERIA
Steve Brady

CHAMPION STEER
Robb Kendrick

Until oil was discovered in the Middle East, Texas was the richest geopolitical subdivision in the world. Texas' wealth, which includes agricultural products (wheat, cotton, and rice) in addition to oil, had to have an outlet to the world. The Port of Houston, opened in 1914, was it. As Houston became Texas' window on the world, the city inevitably focused more and more on cultivating and maintaining its manifold and distant trading contacts. The result is a permanent international community (only New York and San Francisco have more consulates). But once a year in February, for two weeks the city remembers its Texas heritage. Trailriders, 4H Club members, cowboys, and would-be cowboys pour into the city to join thousands of Texas-minded Houstonians, and the Houston Livestock Show and Rodeo sells out the 50,000-seat Astrodome for ten days. Purists may carp about the validity of a rodeo in such a huge arena, but it's the thought – and the spectacle – that counts.

TRAILRIDERS

Hundreds participate in the dozen trailrides – some more than a hundred miles in length – which converge on the city at rodeo time, recreating a lost way-of-life on the open range.

Thaine Manske

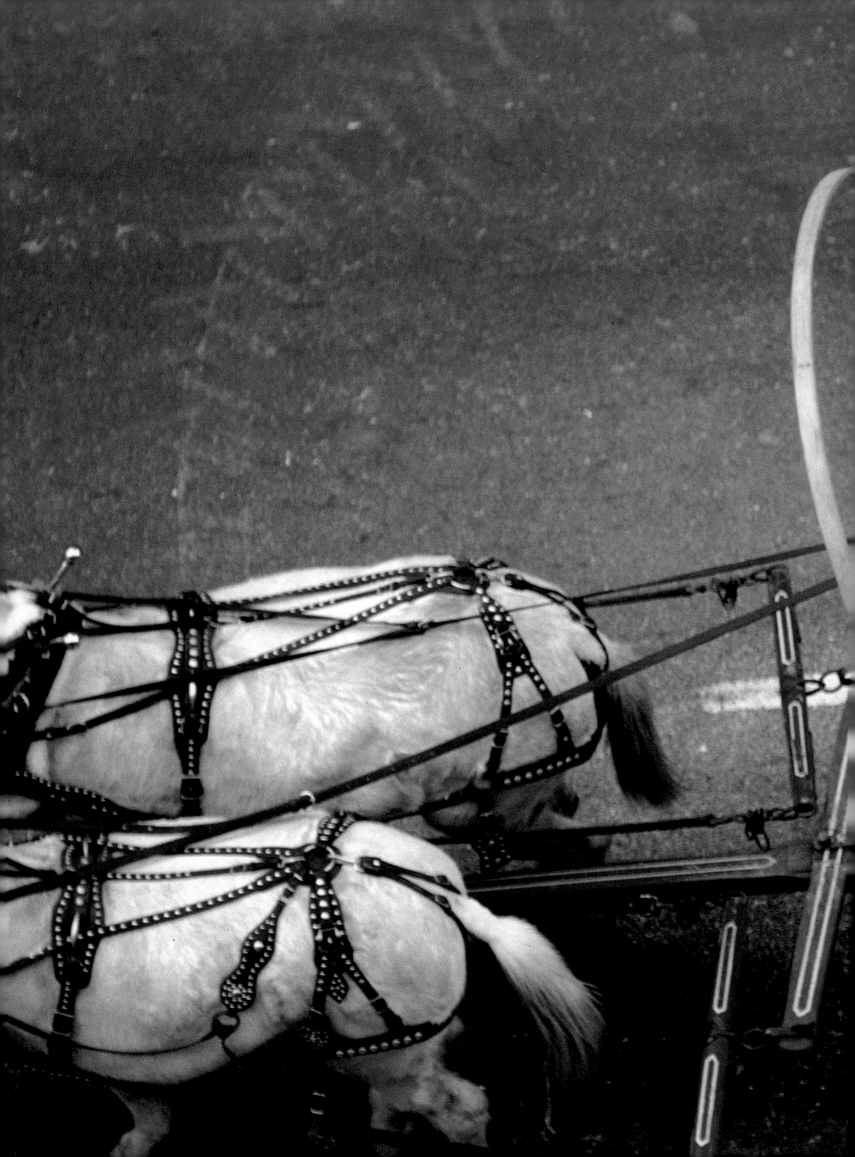

RODEO PARADE
Arthur Meyerson

RODEO PARADE WATCHERS

Arthur Meyerson

CALF SCRAMBLE

Robb Kendrick

TWO COWBOYS

Robb Kendrick

COWBOYS IN THE DOME

Jim Olive

SURVEYOR

Jim Sims

PIPEYARD

Ron Scott

TRAINYARD

Arthur Meyerson

TANK FARM

Arthur Meyerson

RIG MOVING
THROUGH CHANNEL

Jim Sims

COMPAQ COMPUTER
WORKERS
Arthur Meyerson

FIREFIGHTERS
Robb Kendrick

LIFEFLIGHT HELIPAD
Jim Olive

STEEPLEJACKS ON
FOUR LEAF TOWER
Steve Brady

STUDIO
Jim Olive

Against a backdrop of fulltime major performing arts organizations – Houston Grand Opera, the Houston Symphony, Houston Ballet, the Alley Theatre – the city nourishes countless smaller groups. The visual arts especially thrive. Witness the *Fresh Paint* show at the Museum of Fine Arts, through which critic Barbara Rose put the Houston School on the international art map. Witness the Contemporary Arts Museum, the Menil Collection, the Rothko Chapel, Blaffer Gallery, the Rice Museum. In the performing arts, David Gockley brought Houston Grand Opera to the top level internationally, as did Ben Stevenson at Houston Ballet – and as the late Nina Vance did with the Alley Theatre. The Houston Symphony has its own tradition that includes such permanent conductors as Stokowski, Beecham, Previn, Barberolli, and Comissiona.

FRESH PAINT
The Houston School

HOUSTON GRAND OPERA'S 'TURANDOT'

Jim Caldwell

**HOUSTON BALLET'S
'PAPILLON'**

Jim Caldwell

HOUSTON BALLET'S
'PRODIGAL SON
IN RAGTIME'

Jim Caldwell

PLEASE BE SEATED AND ENJOY THE SHOW

THE ORANGE SHOW

The late Jeff McKissack, a postman, worked for two decades on his tribute to the orange. Now operated as a museum and events center by the Orange Show Foundation.

Paul Hester

MUSEUM OF FINE ARTS

Jim Olive

CULLEN AND
ALLEN CENTERS
George O. Jackson, Jr.

If you had to choose one city to study American architecture of the second half of the twentieth century, Houston would have to be it. Since the late 1950's, the city has been a kind of architectural laboratory for the world. Among the architects whose work is on view here are: Ludwig Mies van der Rohe, Philip Johnson and John Burgee, Charles Gwathmey, Charles Moore, I.M. Pei, Cesar Pelli, Stanley Tigerman, Robert Venturi, SITE, Arquitectonica, Skidmore Owings and Merrill, along with well-known local firms such as CRS, Morris*Aubry, 3-D/International, Lloyd Jones Fillpott, and Taft Architects. An impressive list, to be sure. The punchline is that in many cases, the projects built here, represent – by international consensus – the best work by many of these designers. While it is the large structures – the skyscrapers – that are most visible, one of the delights of exploring Houston lies in discovering the countless first-rate, smaller structures, both commercial and residential, which dot the city.

**REPUBLIC BANK CENTER
FRAMED BY
PENNZOIL PLACE**

In 1976 architects Philip Johnson and John Burgee designed Pennzoil Place which broke the International Style highrise mold. Eight years later, they created RepublicBank Center, arguably one of the best of the Post-modern skyscrapers.

Jacques de Selliers

PENNZOIL PLACE

Steve Brady

POST OAK CENTRAL
Joe Baraban

THE OLD GULF BUILDING

Jim Olive

TRANSCO TOWER

Arthur Meyerson

**FOUR OAKS PLACE WITH
THE TRANSCO TOWER**

Jim Sims

NIELS ESPERSON BUILDING
Jim Sims

REPUBLICBANK LOBBY

Richard Payne

**UNIVERSITY OF HOUSTON
SCHOOL OF ARCHITECTURE
LOBBY**

Richard Payne

TRANQUILLITY PARK

One Shell Plaza, the city's first fifty-story building, and Allied Bank Plaza, now the largest building in Houston, are the backdrop for Tranquillity Park.

Richard Payne

ALLIED BANK PLAZA

Joe Aker

REPUBLICBANK

Rocky Kneten

**ANTIOCH BAPTIST CHURCH
FRAMED BY
FOUR ALLEN CENTER**

*The oldest Black church in Houston, now
surrounded by skyscrapers.*

Rocky Kneten

FOUR ALLEN CENTER AND
1600 SMITH IN
CULLEN CENTER

Jacques de Selliers

WORTHAM THEATRE CENTER

Don Glentzer

BEST PRODUCTS SHOWROOM

Joe Aker

TEXAS COMMERCE TOWER
Fred George

THE GLASSELL SCHOOL
Jim Olive

TRANSCO TOWER
ON NEW YEAR'S EVE

George O. Jackson, Jr.

Front Cover
SAM HOUSTON STATUE
Robb Kendrick
© 1985

Back Cover
SAM HOUSTON STATUE
George O. Jackson, Jr.
© 1985

Page 1
SUMMERTIME
Joe Baraban
© 1982

Page 2–3
"RENDEZVOUS HOUSTON,
A CITY IN CONCERT"
Ellis Vener
© 1986

Page 4
SAN JACINTO SUNSET
Joe Baraban
© 1984

Page 6–7
THE DOME
Arthur Meyerson
© 1983

Page 8–9
MEMORIAL PARK
Arthur Meyerson
© 1983

Page 10–11
SUNFISH ON CLEAR LAKE
Sims/Boynton Photography
© 1985

Page 12–13
BLIMP BASE
Sims/Boynton Photography
© 1985

Page 14–15
HOUSTON SHIP CHANNEL
Kent Knudson
© 1981

Page 16–17
RODEO TRAILRIDERS
Jim Olive
© 1984

Page 20–21
FOLK DANCERS
Janice Rubin
© 1985

Page 22–23
LOOKING WEST FROM
DOWNTOWN
Janice Rubin
© 1985

Page 32
SKYLINE FROM I-45
Steve Brady
© 1984

Page 34–35
NIGHT SKYLINE
Rocky Kneten
© 1984

Page 36–37
DOWNTOWN PANORAMA
Lewis Hodnett, Jr.
© 1984

Page 38
SUNSET SKYLINE
George O. Jackson, Jr.
© 1985

Page 39
WEST HOUSTON SKYLINE
George O. Jackson, Jr.
© 1985

Page 40
SAN JACINTO MONUMENT
Arthur Meyerson
© 1984

Page 41
NASA TOURISTS
Jim Caldwell
© 1978

Page 42–43
VISITORS' CENTER
JOHNSON'S SPACE CENTER
Jim Olive
© 1985

Page 44–45
ASTRODOME AT HALFTIME
Bob Gomel
© 1983

Page 46
TRANSCO FOUNTAIN
Steve Brady
© 1985

Page 47
TRANSCO FOUNTAIN
WATER WALL
Steve Brady
© 1985

Page 48–49
DOWNTOWN WITH
DUBUFFET
Bob Gomel
© 1985

Page 50
RICE UNIVERSITY
Ron Scott
© 1983

Page 51
HERMANN HOSPITAL
Steve Brady
© 1982

Page 52–53
HOUSTON ZOO
Chris Kuhlman
© 1986

Page 54
BAYOU BEND
Jim Olive
© 1980

Page 55
GALLERIA
Sims/Boynton Photography
© 1984

Page 56
REFINERY
Ron Scott
© 1982

Page 57
PAGODA IN HERMANN PARK
Sims/Boynton Photography
© 1985

Page 58
SUNSET
George O. Jackson, Jr.
© 1985

Page 59
SKYLINE AT SUNSET
Jim Olive
© 1984

Page 60
DOWNTOWN IN EARLY
MORNING FOG
Sims/Boynton Photography
© 1985

Page 61
SKYLINE IN THE FOG
George O. Jackson, Jr.
© 1985

Page 62
CITY IN THE RAIN
George O. Jackson, Jr.
© 1985

Page 63
CITY WITH A RAINBOW
George O. Jackson, Jr.
© 1985

Page 64–65
MORNING SKY
George O. Jackson, Jr.
© 1986

Page 66
EARLY MORNING OILFIELD
IN SOUTH HOUSTON
Sims/Boynton Photography
© 1985

Page 67
LONGHORN IN WEST
HOUSTON SUNSET
Jim Olive
© 1980

Page 68
GALLERIA COWBOY
Kent Knudson
© 1984

Page 70
ROCKETS
Joe Baraban
© 1985

Page 71
PARTY
Bob Gomel
© 1983

Page 72
KINGWOOD
NEIGHBORHOOD
Steve Brady
© 1982

Page 73
BEFORE THE GAME
Ralf Manstein
© 1984

Page 74–75
WATERSKIING AT THE
SHAMROCK
Bob Gomel
© 1985

Page 76
ON MONTROSE BOULEVARD
Jim Olive
© 1984

Page 77
ICE HOUSE
Robb Kendrick
© 1984

Page 78–79
ON CLEAR LAKE
Sims/Boynton Photography
© 1985

Page 80
WEST HOUSTON
BALLOONISTS
Thaine Manske
© 1984

Page 81
MIDNIGHT MADNESS
BIKE RACE
Robb Kendrick
© 1985

Page 82–83
COUNTRY CLUB GREEN
Sims/Boynton Photography
© 1985

Page 84
RIDING AT GILLEY'S
Bob Gomel
© 1982

Page 85
RIDING IN HERMANN PARK
Ron Scott
© 1983

Page 86
SOFTBALL PLAYERS AT RICE
Jerry Herring
© 1982

Page 87
WALKING IN THE TREES
Jim Sims
© 1985

Page 88–89
GOODE COMPANY
BARBEQUE
Janice Rubin
© 1986

Page 90
RICE BEER BIKE RACE
Jerry Herring
© 1985

Page 92–93
HOUSTON FESTIVAL
Janice Rubin
© 1984

Page 94
GREAT WESTERN AUCTION
Bob Gomel
© 1983

Page 95
TRADE SHOW AT THE DOME
Bob Gomel
© 1981

Page 96
WESTHEIMER COLONY
ARTS FESTIVAL
Mark Green
© 1985

Page 97
WESTHEIMER COLONY
ARTS FESTIVAL
Mark Green
© 1985

Page 98
MARATHON ON
MEMORIAL DRIVE
Thaine Manske
© 1979

Page 99
MARATHON WINDING
THROUGH TOWN
Jim Olive
© 1986

Page 100–101
MARATHON FINISH
Jim Olive
© 1986

Page 102
MILLER OUTDOOR THEATER
F. Carter Smith
© 1984

Page 103
CONCERT
F. Carter Smith
© 1983

This book is dedicated to native Houstonians
Stephen and Matthew Herring.

"Understanding Houston" by Douglas Milburn
is a version of a story which originally appeared
in *Houston City* Magazine, and is printed here
with the kind permission of Lute Harmon,
Publisher, *Houston City* Magazine.

Special thanks to Jan Short for her help in this
book project.

Typesetting by Characters, Inc.
Printed in Japan
Library of Congress Number 86-80649
ISBN 0-917001-04-4

Published by
Herring Press, Inc.
1216 Hawthorne
Houston, Texas 77006
(713) 526-1250

Distributed by
Texas Monthly Press
P.O. Box 1569
Austin, Texas 78767
(512) 476-7085